Quick &
Asian Veg

Cookbook

Over 50 recipes for stir fries, rice, noodles, and appetizers

By Susan Evans

FREE BONUS!

Would you like to receive one of my cookbooks for free? Just leave me on honest review on Amazon and I will send you a digital version of the cookbook of your choice! All you have to do is email me proof of your review and the desired cookbook and format to susan.evans.author@gmail.com. Thank you for your support, and have fun cooking!

THANK YOU 69

INTRODUCTION

Who doesn't enjoy the wonderful and wide-ranging flavors from Asian cuisine? From China, Japan, Thailand, Korea, to Vietnam and more; each region represents a long-standing cooking tradition and history. With classic tangy, sweet, spicy, sour, and savoury dishes, there is something for every mood and taste.

In the following pages you will find Vegetarian-Only Asian recipes that are just as intense and exciting as anything you can find at your local takeout. More importantly, you can impress your family and friends (or just yourself) with the following quick and easy to follow recipes. With over 50 deliciously good stir fries, noodles, rice, curries, and appetizer recipes; you are sure to find a mouth-watering meal that even omnivores will enjoy. Let's get the cooking!

MEASUREMENT CONVERSIONS

Liquid/Volume Measurements (approximate)

1 teaspoon = 1/6 fluid ounce (oz.) = 1/3 tablespoon = 5 ml

1 tablespoon = 1/2 fluid ounce (oz.) = 3 teaspoons = 15 ml

1 fluid ounce (oz.) = 2 tablespoons = 1/8 cup = 30 ml

1/4 cup = 2 fluid ounces (oz.) = 4 tablespoons = 60 ml

1/3 cup = 2⅔ fluid ounces (oz.) = 5 ⅓ tablespoons = 80 ml

1/2 cup = 4 fluid ounces (oz.) = 8 tablespoons = 120 ml

2/3 cup = 5⅓ fluid ounces (oz.) = 10⅔ tablespoons = 160 ml

3/4 cup = 6 fluid ounces (oz.) = 12 tablespoons = 180 ml

7/8 cup = 7 fluid ounces (oz.) = 14 tablespoons = 210 ml

1 cup = 8 fluid ounces (oz.) = 1/2 pint = 240 ml

1 pint = 16 fluid ounces (oz.) = 2 cups = 1/2 quart = 475 ml

1 quart = 4 cups = 32 fluid ounces (oz.) = 2 pints = 950 ml

1 liter = 1.055 quarts = 4.22 cups = 2.11 pints = 1000 ml

1 gallon = 4 quarts = 8 pints = 3.8 liters

Dry/Weight Measurements (approximate)

1 ounce (oz.) = 30 grams (g)

2 ounces (oz.) = 55 grams (g)

3 ounces (oz.) = 85 grams (g)

1/4 pound (lb.) = 4 ounces (oz.) = 125 grams (g)

1/2 pound (lb.) = 8 ounces (oz.) = 240 grams (g)

3/4 pound (lb.) = 12 ounces (oz.) = 375 grams (g)

1 pound (lb.) = 16 ounces (oz.) = 455 grams (g)

2 pounds (lbs.) = 32 ounces (oz.) = 910 grams (g)

1 kilogram (kg) = 2.2 pounds (lbs.) = 1000 gram (g)

STIR FRY

Quick and Easy Thai Tofu

SERVINGS: 4
PREP TIME: 15 min.
TOTAL TIME: 30 min.

Ingredients

- 1 (14 ounce) package firm tofu, cut into 3/4 inch cubes
- 1/3 cup chopped green onion
- 1 1/2 teaspoons olive oil
- 1/2 teaspoon sesame oil
- 1 teaspoon soy sauce
- 2 teaspoons grated fresh ginger root
- 1/4 cup chunky peanut butter
- 3 tablespoons flaked coconut sesame seeds

Instructions

1. In a skillet, heat olive oil and sesame oil over medium-high heat. Reduce heat to medium and cook green onions for 1 minute. Add tofu, and cook 4 minutes, adding soy sauce halfway through. Gently stir in peanut butter and ginger, trying not to break the tofu.
2. Remove from heat and add coconut.
3. Transfer to a serving dish and sprinkle with sesame seeds.

Adzuki Bean Mango with Cilantro Lime Coconut Sauce

SERVINGS: 4
PREP TIME: 15 min.
TOTAL TIME: 30 min.

Ingredients

- 1 cup light coconut milk
- 1/2 cup chopped fresh cilantro
- 1 lime, juiced
- 1 inch piece fresh ginger root, minced
- 1 clove garlic, minced
- 1 tablespoon agave nectar
- 1 tablespoon peanut oil
- 1 red onion, cut into 1 inch long strips
- 1 green bell pepper, cut into 1 inch long strips
- 1/2 cup thinly sliced carrot
- 1 cup canned adzuki beans, drained
- 2 small mangos - peeled and cut into strips

Instructions

1. In a food processor or blender, blend the coconut milk, cilantro, lime juice, ginger, garlic, and agave nectar until smooth. Set aside.
2. In a wok or large skillet, heat peanut oil over medium-high heat. Cook onion, bell pepper, and carrot in the hot oil for about 10 minutes, or until the carrot is tender. Add adzuki beans and mango. Stir and cook until the mango is hot.
3. Pour the sauce over the top and serve.

Veggies and Tofu in Peanut Sauce

SERVINGS: 4
PREP TIME: 10 min.
TOTAL TIME: 20 min.

Ingredients

- 1 tablespoon peanut oil
- 1 small head broccoli, chopped
- 1 small red bell pepper, chopped
- 5 fresh mushrooms, sliced
- 1 pound firm tofu, cubed
- 1/2 cup peanut butter
- 1/2 cup hot water
- 2 tablespoons vinegar
- 2 tablespoons soy sauce
- 1 1/2 tablespoons molasses ground cayenne pepper to taste

Instructions

1. In a large skillet or wok, heat oil over medium-high heat. Sauté broccoli, red bell pepper, mushrooms and tofu for 5 minutes.
2. Combine peanut butter, hot water, vinegar, soy sauce, molasses and cayenne pepper in a small bowl. Pour over tofu and vegetables. Simmer for 3 to 5 minutes, or until vegetables are tender crisp.
3. Serve.

Orange Tofu Stir-Fry

SERVINGS: 4
PREP TIME: 15 min.
TOTAL TIME: 30 min.

Ingredients

- 1/4 cup vegetable oil
- 1/4 cup corn-starch
- 1 (16 ounce) package firm tofu, drained and cut into strips
- 2 tablespoons soy sauce
- 1/2 cup orange juice
- 1/4 cup warm water
- 1 tablespoon sugar
- 1 teaspoon chili paste
- 1 teaspoon corn-starch
- 1 tablespoon vegetable oil
- 2 carrots, sliced

Instructions

1. Place 1/4 cup oil in a wok over medium-high heat. Place corn-starch in a dish and coat tofu strips on all sides by pressing on corn-starch.
   Stir-fry in wok for 5 minutes, or until golden brown on all sides. On paper towels, drain tofu. Let the wok cool and wipe clean.
2. Mix the soy sauce, orange juice, water, sugar, chili paste, and corn-starch in a bowl until smooth.
3. In the wok, heat the remaining 1 tablespoon oil and stir-fry the carrots until tender. In the center of the carrots form a well and pour in the mix. Bring to a boil. Place tofu in the wok and continue cooking until completely coated with sauce.

Sweet and Sour Seitan

Ingredients

- 2 teaspoons canola oil
- 1 pound chicken style seitan
- 2 cloves garlic, minced
- 1 large bell pepper, cut in strips
- 1 large onion, chopped
- 1 (20 ounce) can pineapple chunks with juice
- 1 cup pineapple juice
- 1/3 cup brown sugar
- 1/4 cup cider vinegar
- 2 1/2 tablespoons soy sauce
- 2 tablespoons corn-starch

Instructions

1. In a large skillet, heat oil over medium heat. Add seitan and cook until browned, stirring occasionally.
2. Add bell pepper, onion, and garlic. Stir and cook until crisp but tender.
3. Stir in pineapple juice, brown sugar, vinegar, soy sauce and corn-starch. Reduce heat to low and stir until thick. Just before serving, mix in pineapple chunks.

Veggie Stir-Fry

SERVINGS: 4
PREP TIME: 20 min.
TOTAL TIME: 30 min.

Ingredients

- 1 teaspoon corn-starch
- 2 tablespoons water
- 1 tablespoon soy sauce
- 2 tablespoons olive oil
- 3 tablespoons vegetable oil
- 1 carrot, sliced
- 1 red bell pepper, chopped
- 1 zucchini, sliced
- 2/3 cup fresh corn kernels
- 1 clove crushed garlic
- 4 green onions, sliced
- 1 1/3 cups bean sprouts

Instructions

1. In a small bowl, whisk the corn-starch and water together. Add the soy sauce and olive oil. Set aside.
2. Heat the vegetable oil in a wok or skillet over medium-high heat. Sauté the carrot, pepper, and zucchini in the oil for about 5 minutes. Add and stir in the corn, garlic, green onions, and bean sprouts. Pour in the soy sauce mixture and stir, cook for about 5 minutes, or until vegetables are crisp but tender.
3. Serve immediately.

Tofu Peanut Stir-Fry

SERVINGS: 8
PREP TIME: 15 min.
TOTAL TIME: 30 min.

Ingredients

- 1 teaspoon vegetable oil
- 1 (16 ounce) package frozen stir-fry vegetables
- 1/2 teaspoon minced fresh ginger
- salt and pepper to taste
- 2 eggs, beaten
- 1 cup corn-starch salt and pepper to taste
- 1 (14 ounce) package firm tofu, drained and cubed
- 1/2 cup vegetable oil
- 3/4 cup peanut sauce
- 1/4 cup chopped peanuts

Instructions

1. In a large skillet or wok, heat oil over medium heat and cook vegetables until tender. Stir in ginger and season with salt and pepper. Remove vegetables from the skillet, and set aside.
2. Place eggs in a bowl and in a separate bowl, mix the corn-starch, salt, and pepper. Dip the tofu cubes in the egg and then dip in the corn-starch mix to coat.
3. Heat the rest of the oil over medium heat in the skillet or wok, and cook the coated tofu for 5 minutes, or until golden brown. Mix in the peanuts and peanut sauce. Cook and stir until sauce is thick and tofu is well-coated.
4. Serve with the vegetables.

Ginger Veggie Stir-Fry

SERVINGS: 6
PREP TIME: 10 min.
TOTAL TIME: 20 min.

Ingredients

- 1 tablespoon corn-starch
- 1 1/2 cloves garlic, crushed
- 2 teaspoons chopped fresh ginger root, divided
- 1/4 cup vegetable oil, divided
- 1 small head broccoli, cut into florets
- 1/2 cup snow peas
- 3/4 cup julienned carrots
- 1/2 cup halved green beans
- 2 tablespoons soy sauce
- 2 1/2 tablespoons water
- 1/4 cup chopped onion
- 1/2 tablespoon salt

Instructions

1. Combine corn-starch, garlic, 1 teaspoon ginger, and 2 tablespoons vegetable oil in a large bowl until corn-starch is dissolved. Add broccoli, snow peas, carrots, and green beans, and toss to lightly coat.
2. In a large skillet or wok, heat the remaining 2 tablespoons of oil over medium heat. Cook vegetables in oil for 2 minutes, stirring constantly. Mix in soy sauce, water, onion, salt, and remaining 1 teaspoon ginger. Cook until vegetables are crisp but tender.

Vegetable and Tofu Stir-fry

SERVINGS: 4
PREP TIME: 15 min.
TOTAL TIME: 45 min.

Ingredients

- 1 tablespoon vegetable oil
- 1/2 medium onion, sliced
- 2 cloves garlic, finely chopped
- 1 tablespoon fresh ginger root, finely chopped
- 1 (16 ounce) package tofu, drained and cut into cubes
- 1/2 cup water
- 4 tablespoons rice wine vinegar
- 2 tablespoons honey
- 2 tablespoons soy sauce
- 2 teaspoons corn-starch dissolved in
- 2 tablespoons water
- 1 carrot, peeled and sliced
- 1 green bell pepper, seeded and cut into strips
- 1 cup baby corn, drained and cut into pieces
- 1 small head bok choy, chopped
- 2 cups fresh mushrooms, chopped
- 1 1/4 cups bean sprouts
- 1 cup bamboo shoots, drained and chopped
- 1/2 teaspoon crushed red pepper
- 2 medium green onions, thinly sliced diagonally

Instructions

1. In a large skillet, heat oil over medium-high heat. Stir in onions and cook for 1 minute. Add garlic and ginger and cook for 30 seconds. Mix in tofu and cook until golden brown
2. Add carrots, bell pepper and baby corn and cook for 2 minutes. Stir in bok choy, mushrooms, bean sprouts, bamboo shoots, and crushed red pepper. Cook until heated through. Remove skillet from heat.
3. Combine water, rice wine vinegar, honey, and soy sauce in a small saucepan, and bring to a simmer. Cook for 2 minutes. Stir in corn-

starch and water mix and simmer until sauce is thick. Pour sauce over tofu and vegetables. Garnish with scallions.

Braised Tofu

SERVINGS: 4
PREP TIME: 10 min.
TOTAL TIME: 30 min.

Ingredients

- 1 (14 ounce) package firm tofu
- 3 teaspoons sesame oil, divided
- 1 (8 ounce) can water chestnuts, drained
- 3 ounces fresh shiitake mushrooms, stems removed
- 1 1/2 cups snow peas, trimmed
- 1/2 teaspoon oyster flavored sauce
- 1 cup water

Instructions

1. Slice tofu block into three long lengthwise blocks. Wrap each in paper towels and squeeze out excess water.
2. Spray large skillet with cooking spray, and add 2 teaspoons of sesame oil. Once oil is hot, add the tofu to skillet. Fry for about 5 minutes on each side, or until lightly browned.
3. Remove tofu from skillet and slice into cubes. Add remaining sesame oil to the skillet and fry the water chestnuts, mushrooms and snow peas. Mix water and oyster sauce and add along with the tofu to the skillet. Cover and cook for about 10 minutes over low heat.

RICE

Stir Fried Sesame Vegetables with Rice

SERVINGS: 4
PREP TIME: 15 min.
TOTAL TIME: 30 min.

Ingredients

- 1 1/2 cups vegetable broth
- 3/4 cup uncooked long-grain white rice
- 1 tablespoon margarine
- 1 tablespoon sesame seeds
- 2 tablespoons peanut oil
- 1/2 pound fresh asparagus, trimmed and cut into 1 inch pieces
- 1 large red bell pepper, cut into 1 inch pieces
- 1 large yellow onion, sliced
- 2 cups sliced mushrooms
- 2 teaspoons minced fresh ginger root
- 1 teaspoon minced garlic
- 3 tablespoons soy sauce
- 1 tablespoon sesame oil

Instructions

1. Preheat oven to 350 degrees F (175 degrees C).
2. Combine broth, rice, and margarine in a saucepan. Cover and boil over high heat. Reduce heat to low and simmer for 15 minutes, or until all liquid is absorbed.
3. Place sesame seeds on a small baking sheet and bake in oven for 5 to 6 minutes, or until golden brown. Set aside.
4. In a large skillet or wok, heat peanut oil over medium-high heat until very hot. Mix in asparagus, bell pepper, onion, mushrooms, ginger and garlic and stir-fry 4 to 5 minutes, or until vegetables are crisp but tender. Stir in soy-sauce and cook for 30 seconds. Remove from heat and stir in sesame oil and sesame seeds.
5. Serve over rice.

Sweet and Sour Veggies and Tofu

SERVINGS: 4
PREP TIME: 15 min.
TOTAL TIME: 40 min.

Ingredients

- 3 cups water
- 1 1/2 cups long-grain brown rice
- 1 pound firm tofu
- 1/4 cup unsweetened pineapple juice
- 2 tablespoons fresh lemon juice
- 2 tablespoons ketchup
- 2 tablespoons maple syrup
- 2 tablespoons tamari
- 1 tablespoon dark sesame oil
- 2 1/4 teaspoons arrowroot powder
- 2 1/2 teaspoons grated ginger
- 2 tablespoons vegetable oil
- 1 onion, thinly sliced
- 1 carrots, sliced diagonally
- 4 ounces fresh green beans, cut into 1-inch lengths
- 1 large chopped red bell pepper
- 8 ounces fresh mushrooms, sliced
- 1 zucchini, cut into 1/2-inch slices
- 1 cup pineapple chunks

Instructions

1. Bring 2 cups of the water to a boil in a medium saucepan. Reduce heat. Add rice and simmer for 30 to 40 minutes, or until the rice is tender and water is absorbed. Transfer to serving plate and keep warm.
2. Squeeze out excess water from the tofu and then cut it into 1/2-inch cubes.
3. Whisk the pineapple juice, lemon juice, ketchup, maple syrup, tamari, sesame oil, arrowroot, and ginger together in a small bowl.

[17]

4. Heat vegetable oil over medium-high heat in a wok or large skillet. Add the onion, carrot, green beans, bell pepper, mushrooms, and zucchini and stir-fry 3 to 5 minutes or until tender.
5. Add pineapple juice mix, tofu and pineapple. Cook until the sauce is thick, about 2 minutes, stirring often.
6. Spoon veggies and sauce over rice and serve.

Korean Bibimbap

SERVINGS: 3
PREP TIME: 20 min.
TOTAL TIME: 40 min.

Ingredients

- 2 tablespoons sesame oil
- 1 cup carrot, cut like matchsticks
- 1 cup zucchini, cut like matchsticks
- 1/2 (14 ounce) can bean sprouts, drained
- 6 ounces canned bamboo shoots, drained
- 1 (4.5 ounce) can sliced mushrooms, drained
- 1/8 teaspoon salt to taste
- 2 cups cooked and cooled rice
- 1/3 cup sliced green onions
- 2 tablespoons soy sauce
- 1/4 teaspoon ground black pepper
- 1 tablespoon butter
- 3 eggs
- 3 teaspoons sweet red chili sauce, to taste

Instructions

1. Heat sesame oil over medium heat in a large skillet. Stir in carrot and zucchini for about 5 minutes or until vegetables begin to soften. Stir in bean sprouts, bamboo shoots, and mushrooms. Cook for about 5 minutes until carrots are tender. Season with salt to taste and set aside.
2. In the same skillet, stir cooked rice, green onions, soy sauce, and black pepper until rice is hot.
3. In a different skillet over medium heat, melt butter and gently fry, turning once until yolks are slightly runny but egg whites are firm, about 3 minutes for each egg.
4. Divide hot cooked rice mixture between serving bowls and top each with 1/3 of the vegetable mixture and a fried egg. Serve sweet red chili sauce on the side for mixing.

Chinese Fried Rice

SERVINGS: 4
PREP TIME: 10 min.
TOTAL TIME: 30 min.

Ingredients

- 1 1/2 cups uncooked instant rice
- 1 tablespoon sesame oil
- soy sauce, to taste
- 2 eggs, beaten
- 1 teaspoon finely chopped fresh ginger root
- 1/4 cup finely chopped green onions

Instructions

1. Bring water to a boil in a medium pan. Stir in rice and cover. Remove from heat and let stand 5 minutes. Fluff with a fork and drain excess water.
2. In a large skillet, heat oil over medium heat. Stir in rice and soy sauce. Quickly heat then transfer rice to a bowl.
3. In the same skillet, scramble the eggs and stir in rice. Mix in ginger and green onions. Heat through and serve.

Vegetable Fried Rice

SERVINGS: 8
PREP TIME: 15 min.
TOTAL TIME: 30 min. + chilling

Ingredients

- 1 1/2 cups uncooked long-grain white rice
- 3 cups water
- 2 tablespoons vegetable oil, divided
- 1/3 cup chopped onion
- 1 clove garlic, peeled and minced
- 5 eggs, beaten
- 1/4 cup soy sauce, divided
- 2 stalks celery, thinly sliced
- 4 ounces mushrooms, sliced
- 1 green bell pepper, chopped
- 1 (8 ounce) can bamboo shoots, drained
- 2 carrots, shredded
- 3/4 cup snow peas
- 3 green onions, sliced

Instructions

1. In a medium saucepan, combine rice and water. Bring to a boil. Reduce heat to low, cover, and simmer for 20 minutes, or until rice is tender. Transfer to a medium bowl and chill for at least 1 hour in a refrigerator.
2. In a medium skillet, heat 1 tablespoon of oil over medium heat. Stir in the onion and garlic, and cook until tender.
3. Combine eggs and 1 tablespoon soy sauce in skillet and cook until no longer runny. Remove onion, garlic, and eggs from heat, and set aside. Chop large chunks of egg into smaller pieces.
4. In a large skillet, heat remaining oil over medium heat. Stir in the celery, mushrooms, and green pepper; cooking until firm but tender. Stir in rice, bamboo shoots, carrots, and snow peas; season with remaining soy sauce. Cook and stir for 5 minutes, or until rice is heated through.
5. Mix in onion, garlic, and eggs. Serve.

Bean Curd and Devil Fried Rice

SERVINGS: 6
PREP TIME: 30 min.
TOTAL TIME: 1 hour

Ingredients

- 6 sticks dried bean curd
- 1 tablespoon shredded black fungus
- 7 dried black mushrooms
- boiling water
- 3 1/4 cups water
- 2 cups basmati rice
- 1 tablespoon butter or oil
- 4 eggs, beaten
- 3 tablespoons vegetable oil, or as needed
- 1 cup cubed carrots
- 1 cup chopped yellow onion
- 4 tablespoons minced fresh ginger root
- 4 tablespoons minced garlic
- 1/2 cup thinly sliced green onions
- 1 cup frozen peas
- 3 tablespoons tamari
- 2 tablespoons sesame oil fresh
- ground black pepper

Instructions

1. In a bowl, place the dried bean curd and cover with boiling water. In a different bowl, place shredded black fungus and dried black mushrooms, and cover with boiling water. Let the bean curd, black fungus, and dried black mushrooms to soak for about 20 minutes, or until rehydrated
2. Place 3 1/4 cups of water with rice in a saucepan and bring to a boil over high heat. Cover with a lid, and reduce heat to low. Cook for 5 minutes, and remove from heat. Let stand for about 20 minutes, leaving the cover on.
3. Melt butter over medium-high heat in a non-stick skillet. Scramble eggs and dump into a bowl. Chop them into small pieces with edge of a wooden spoon.

4. Combine carrot, onion, garlic, and ginger in a bowl. In a different bowl, combine green onions and frozen peas. Drain water from the bean curd, fungus and mushrooms. Cut bean curd into quarter-inch rings, and slice fungus and mushrooms.
5. Heat a skillet or wok over high heat for about 1 minute. Add 3 tablespoons of vegetable oil. Wait 30 seconds, add the bowl of carrot, onion, garlic, and ginger. Cook and stir frequently, making sure not to let the garlic burn. Stir in the rice, eggs, and season with tamari, sesame oil, and fresh black pepper.

Pineapple Fried Rice

SERVINGS: 8
PREP/ TOTAL TIME: 35 min.

Ingredients

- 1 (8 ounce) can crushed pineapple with juice
- 4 cups water
- 2 cups white rice
- 1 tablespoon peanut or walnut oil
- 2 eggs, beaten
- 1/2 teaspoon sesame oil
- 1 (12 ounce) package tofu, diced
- 3/4 cup chopped mushrooms
- 3 tablespoons soy sauce
- 3 green onions, thinly sliced
- 1 cup diced carrots

Instructions

1. Drain juice from can of crushed pineapple and pour into a cup.
2. Combine pineapple liquid with 3 cups water in a medium saucepan, and bring to a boil. Add rice and bring mixture to boil. Cover and reduce heat to simmer. Cook 25 to 30 minutes, or until rice is soft and tender.
3. Heat the 1 tablespoon walnut or peanut oil in a non-stick wok or skillet. Add eggs and cook until set, making sure not to stir. Slide eggs out of wok and to a plate. Cut eggs in narrow strips. Heat the sesame oil in the same wok and stir fry tofu with the mushrooms, soy sauce, green onions, and carrots for about 4 minutes. Stir in cooked rice, pineapple, and egg strips. Heat until all ingredients are heated through.

Swimming Angels

SERVINGS: 4
PREP TIME: 15 min.
TOTAL TIME: 45 min.

Ingredients

- 2 cups uncooked sushi (sticky) or medium-grain rice
- 4 cups water
- 2/3 cup peanut butter
- 1 cup hot water
- 2 tablespoons soy sauce
- 2 tablespoons rice vinegar
- 3 tablespoons white sugar
- 3 cloves garlic, minced
- 3 green onions, chopped
- 1/4 teaspoon red pepper flakes
- 1 (10 ounce) bag baby spinach leaves
- 1 (8 ounce) package baked tofu, cut into bite-size pieces

Instructions

1. In a saucepan, combine rice and 4 cups of water and bring to a boil. Cover and reduce heat to low. Simmer about 20 minutes, or until rice is tender and water is absorbed.
2. In a separate pan, whisk peanut butter, 1 cup hot water, soy sauce, rice vinegar, sugar, garlic, green onions and red pepper flakes. Bring to a simmer over medium heat, cooking and stirring occasionally. Add hot water 1/4 cup at a time to maintain consistency.
3. In a large pot, bring about 1 inch of water to a boil. Place spinach and tofu in a steamer basket, setting over boiling water. Cover and steam for 7 minutes, or until spinach is wilted and tofu is heated through.
4. Place spinach and tofu over white rice and cover in peanut sauce.

Teriyaki Wraps

SERVINGS: 4
PREP TIME: 10 min.
TOTAL TIME: 25 min.

Ingredients

- 1 cup uncooked long grain white rice
- 2 cups water
- 2 tablespoons olive oil
- 1 onion, chopped
- 1 red bell pepper, chopped
- 1 small zucchini, chopped
- 1 small yellow squash, chopped
- 1 1/4 cups teriyaki sauce
- 3 tablespoons soy sauce
- 2 teaspoons garlic powder
- 1/2 teaspoon salt
- 1 teaspoon ground black pepper
- 4 (10 inch) whole wheat tortillas

Instructions

1. Bring 2 cups of water to a boil in a saucepan. Add rice, reduce heat, cover, and simmer for 20 minutes.
2. In a large skillet, heat olive over medium heat. Sauté onion, bell pepper, zucchini, and yellow squash until onions are tender. Stir in the teriyaki sauce. When the vegetables are tender, add in the cooked rice, soy sauce, garlic powder, salt and pepper. Stir and simmer for 3 to 5 minutes.
3. Place 1/4 of the rice and vegetables in each tortilla, and roll.

Lentils and Beans Spicy Rice

SERVINGS: 6
PREP TIME: 10 min.
TOTAL TIME: 45 min.

Ingredients

- 2 1/2 cups vegetable broth
- 2 green onions, chopped
- 1 cup frozen green peas
- 1/2 teaspoon salt
- 1 pinch garam masala
- 1 pinch turmeric powder ground cayenne pepper, to taste
- 1 cup basmati rice
- 1 1/2 tablespoons butter
- 10 large fresh mushrooms, chopped
- 5 cloves garlic, chopped
- 1/2 green bell pepper, chopped
- 1/2 red bell pepper, chopped
- 1 teaspoon garam masala
- 1 pinch turmeric powder and cayenne pepper, to taste
- 1/2 cup dry red lentils
- 3/4 cup vegetable broth
- 1/2 cup almond slivers
- 1 bunch cilantro sprigs

Instructions

1. Bring 2 1/2 cups broth to a boil in a pot. Mix in green onions and peas. Season with salt, 1 pinch garam masala, 1 pinch turmeric, and cayenne pepper, to taste Stir in basmati rice and reduce heat to low. Cover and simmer 20 minutes.
2. In a wok, melt butter over medium-high heat. Cook and stir in the mushrooms and garlic until lightly browned. Add green bell pepper, red bell pepper, and season with 1 teaspoon garam masala, 1 pinch turmeric, and cayenne pepper; to taste. Stir in lentils and 3/4 cup broth. Reduce heat to low. Cook 20 minutes or until lentils are tender, stirring occasionally.

3. Cook almonds in a skillet over medium heat, until lightly browned, stirring frequently. Remove from heat, and set aside.
4. Increase heat of wok to medium. Mix rice in wok with the vegetables and lentils. Cook and stir until liquid is evaporated.
5. Garnish with toasted almonds and cilantro sprigs. Serve.

Indonesian Fried Rice

SERVINGS: 4
PREP TIME: 25 min.
TOTAL TIME: 40 min.

Ingredients

- 1/2 cup uncooked long grain white rice
- 1 cup water
- 2 teaspoons sesame oil
- 1 small onion, chopped
- 2 cloves garlic, minced
- 1 green chile pepper, chopped
- 1 small carrot, sliced
- 1 stalk celery, sliced
- 2 tablespoons kecap manis
- 2 tablespoons tomato sauce
- 2 tablespoons soy sauce
- 1/4 cucumber, sliced
- 4 eggs

Instructions

1. In a pot, combine rice and water and bring to a boil. Cover, reduce heat to low, and simmer for 20 minutes.
2. In a wok, heat oil and cook the onion, garlic, and green chile until tender. Mix in the carrot and celery. Stir in rice, kecap manis, tomato sauce, and soy sauce. Cook for 1 minute, until heated through. Transfer to bowls, and garnish with cucumber slices.
3. Place eggs in the wok, and cook until set. Serve over the rice and vegetable

Cashew and Asparagus Rice Pilaf

SERVINGS: 8
PREP TIME: 15 min.
TOTAL TIME: 45 min.

Ingredients

- 1/4 cup butter
- 2 ounces uncooked spaghetti, broken
- 1/4 cup minced onion
- 1/2 teaspoon minced garlic
- 1 1/4 cups uncooked jasmine rice
- 2 1/4 cups vegetable
- broth salt and pepper to taste
- 1/2 pound fresh asparagus, trimmed and cut into 2 inch pieces
- 1/2 cup cashew halves

Instructions

1. In a medium saucepan, melt butter over medium-low heat. Increase heat to medium, and stir in spaghetti, cooking until coated with the melted butter and lightly browned.
2. In saucepan, stir onion and garlic, cooking for about 2 minutes, or until tender. Stir in jasmine rice, and cook 5 minutes. Pour in vegetable broth, and season with salt and pepper. Bring to a boil, cover, and cook 20 minutes, until rice is tender and liquid is absorbed.
3. In a separate medium saucepan, place asparagus and cover with water. Bring to a boil, and cook until firm but tender.
4. Mix asparagus and cashew into the rice mix.
5. Serve warm.

Egg Fried Rice

SERVINGS: 4
PREP TIME: 5 min.
TOTAL TIME: 20 min.

Ingredients

- 1 cup water
- 1/2 teaspoon salt
- 2 tablespoons soy sauce
- 1 cup uncooked instant rice
- 1 teaspoon vegetable oil
- 1/2 onion, finely chopped
- 1/2 cup green beans
- 1 egg, lightly beaten
- 1/4 teaspoon ground black pepper

Instructions

1. Bring water, salt and soy sauce to a boil in a saucepan. Add rice and stir. Remove from heat, cover, and let stand for 5 minutes.
2. In a medium skillet or wok, heat oil over medium heat. Sauté onions and green beans for 2 to 3 minutes. Add egg and fry for 2 minutes, scrambling during cooking
3. Stir in the cooked rice, combine, and sprinkle with pepper.

NOODLES

Malay Style Spicy Noodles

SERVINGS: 4
PREP TIME: 15 min.
TOTAL TIME: 40 min.

Ingredients

- 1 (12 ounce) package uncooked egg noodles
- 3 tablespoons olive oil
- 1 teaspoon finely chopped garlic
- 1/2 bunch fresh spinach, stems removed, chopped
- 1/4 cup chile paste
- 3 tablespoons ketchup
- 1 egg
- 1/2 teaspoon white sugar
- 1/4 cup water
- salt and pepper, to taste
- 1/2 cup fresh bean sprouts
- 1/2 cup green peas

Instructions

1. Boil lightly salted water in a large pot. Add the egg noodles and cook for 6 to 8 minutes, until al dente. Drain.
2. In a skillet, heat the oil over medium heat, and sauté the garlic for 1 minute. Stir in spinach, and cook for another 1 minute. Add cooked egg noodles, chile paste, and ketchup, and toss until well coated.
3. Make a hole in the center of the noodle mix. Place egg in center and scramble. Just before egg is finished cooking, toss with the noodles.
4. In the skillet, mix sugar and enough water to keep the mixture moist. Season with salt and pepper. Continue to cook, about 6 minutes, stirring constantly. Add the sprouts and peas, cooking and stirring for about 4 minutes, until heated through.

Vegetarian Pho

Ingredients

- 64 ounces homemade or low-sodium vegetable broth
- 6 green onions, thinly sliced
- 1 tablespoon fresh ginger, peeled and grated
- Salt to taste
- 1 1/2 tablespoon butter
- 6 ounces shiitake mushrooms, tough stems removed
- 1 1/2 tablespoon hoisin sauce
- 2 teaspoons sesame oil
- 14 ounces rice noodles, cooked according to package instructions
- 8 ounces bean sprouts
- 2 jalapeño peppers, thinly sliced
- Fresh cilantro, basil, lime wedges, hoisin sauce, and chili garlic sauce or sriracha for serving.

Instructions

1. Combine vegetable broth, green onion, grated ginger, and salt in a large pot. Bring to a boil, reduce the heat, and simmer for 15 minutes.
2. In a large skillet, melt the butter over medium heat. Add mushrooms and sauté for about 6 minutes, or until tender, frequently stirring. Stir in hoisin and sesame oil and cook until the sauce is thick and mushrooms are coated, about 1 minute. Remove from heat.
3. Fill each serving bowl with the ginger broth. Add bean sprouts, sliced jalapeños, shiitake mushrooms, fresh basil, and cilantro. Serve with lime wedges, hoisin, and chili garlic sauce.

Vegetable Cashew Sauté

SERVINGS: 8
PREP TIME: 10 min.
TOTAL TIME: 30 min.

Ingredients

- 1 (16 ounce) package whole wheat rotini pasta
- 2 tablespoons dark sesame oil
- 1/4 cup soy sauce
- 1/4 cup balsamic vinegar
- 2 tablespoons white sugar
- 1/4 cup dark sesame oil
- 3 cups chopped broccoli
- 1 cup chopped carrots
- 1 cup chopped red bell pepper
- 2 cups chopped fresh shiitake mushrooms
- 1 cup shelled edamame (green soybeans)
- 3/4 cup chopped unsalted cashew nuts

Instructions

1. Boil lightly salted water in a large pot. Cook rotini for 10 to 12 minutes, until al dente. Drain.
2. Mix 2 tablespoons sesame oil, soy sauce, vinegar, and sugar in a small bowl.
3. In a skillet, heat 1/4 cup sesame oil over medium heat. Stir in the broccoli, carrots, red bell pepper, mushrooms, shelled edamame, and cashews. Add and mix in the sesame oil sauce. Cover, and cook for 5 minutes, or until vegetables are crisp but tender.
4. Serve over the cooked pasta.

Raw Pad Thai

Ingredients

- 2 zucchini, ends trimmed
- 2 carrots
- 1 head red cabbage, thinly sliced
- 1 red bell pepper, thinly sliced
- 1/2 cup bean sprouts
- 3/4 cup raw almond butter
- 2 oranges, juiced
- 2 tablespoons raw honey
- 1 tablespoon minced fresh ginger root
- 1 tablespoon Nama Shoyu (raw soy sauce)
- 1 tablespoon unpasteurized miso
- 1 clove garlic, minced
- 1/4 teaspoon cayenne pepper

Instructions

1. To create "noodles", slice zucchini lengthwise with a vegetable peeler. Place on serving plates.
2. Slice carrots in a similar manner to step 1.
3. In a large bowl, combine carrots, cabbage, red bell pepper, and bean sprouts.
4. In a bowl, whisk together almond butter, orange juice, honey, ginger, Nama Shoyu, miso, garlic, and cayenne pepper.
5. Pour half of the sauce into cabbage mix and toss to coat.
6. Top zucchini "noodles" with cabbage mixture.
7. Pour remaining sauce over each portion.

Choy, Shiitakes Rice Noodle with Chile

SERVINGS: 4
PREP/TOTAL TIME: 20 min.

Ingredients

- 2 1/2 tablespoons soy sauce
- 3 tablespoons sake or sherry
- 2 tablespoons balsamic vinegar
- 2 teaspoons white sugar
- 3 tablespoons water
- 2 teaspoons corn-starch
- 1 tablespoon canola oil
- 2 tablespoons dark sesame oil
- 2 cloves garlic, sliced
- 6 whole dried red chile peppers, seeded and diced
- 1 tablespoon minced fresh ginger root
- 1 medium head bok choy, cut into 1 1/2 inch strips
- 20 fresh shiitake mushrooms, stemmed and quartered
- 8 green onions, halved lengthwise
- 2 (9 ounce) packages fresh rice noodles
- 2 tablespoons sesame seeds, toasted

Instructions

1. In a small bowl, whisk together soy sauce, sake or sherry, vinegar, sugar, water and corn-starch.
2. Heat the oils over high heat in a large skillet or wok. When oil is almost smoking, add garlic and hot peppers. After 10 seconds, remove skillet or wok from heat.
3. Reduce heat to medium-high and return skillet or wok to heat. Add ginger, bok choy, shiitakes, and green onions. Cook for 3 minutes over high heat, constantly stirring.
4. Add the fresh or soaked rice noodles and the soy sauce mixture to the skillet or wok. Cook 2 minutes more or until the noodles are tender and hot. Top noodles with toasted sesame seeds and serve immediately.

Veggie Pad Thai

SERVINGS: 8
PREP TIME: 20 min.
TOTAL TIME: 40 min. + soaking

Ingredients

- 1 pound dried rice noodles
- 2 tablespoons vegetable oil
- 4 eggs, beaten
- 2 tablespoons peanut oil
- 1 1/2 cups peanut butter
- 1/3 cup water
- 1/3 cup soy sauce
- 1 cup milk
- 1 1/4 cups brown sugar
- 1/3 cup lemon juice
- 2 tablespoons garlic powder
- 1 tablespoon paprika cayenne pepper to taste
- 1 pound mung bean sprouts
- 1 cup shredded carrots
- 1/4 cup chopped green onions
- 1/2 cup chopped, unsalted dry-roasted peanuts
- 1 lime, cut into wedges

Instructions

1. In a large bowl of hot water, submerge the rice noodles for an hour.
2. In a large skillet, pour 1/2 tablespoon of oil and add eggs. Scramble into medium-sized pieces. Transfer to plate and set aside.
3. In a saucepan, combine peanut oil, peanut butter, water, soy sauce, milk, brown sugar, and lemon juice. Mix and season with garlic powder and paprika. Heat sauce until smooth. Season with cayenne pepper.
4. Drain noodles. They should be flexible, but relatively firm. In a large saucepan or wok, heat remaining 1 1/2 tablespoons vegetable oil. Cook noodles in oil, constantly stirring for about 2 minutes until tender. Stir in peanut sauce, sprouts, carrots, scallions, ground

peanuts, and the scrambled eggs. Cook over low heat for about 5 minutes, or until vegetables are tender but crisp.

5. Serve immediately, and garnish with lime wedges.

Sukhothai Pad Thai

SERVINGS: 8
PREP TIME: 10 min.
TOTAL TIME: 20 min.

Ingredients

- 1/2 cup white sugar
- 1/2 cup distilled white vinegar
- 1/4 cup soy sauce
- 2 tablespoons tamarind pulp
- 1 (12 ounce) package dried rice noodles
- 1/2 cup vegetable oil
- 1 1/2 teaspoons minced garlic
- 4 eggs
- 1 (12 ounce) package firm tofu, cut into 1/2 inch strips
- 1 1/2 tablespoons white sugar
- 1 1/2 teaspoons salt
- 1 1/2 cups ground peanuts
- 1 1/2 teaspoons ground, dried oriental radish
- 1/2 cup chopped fresh chives
- 1 tablespoon paprika
- 2 cups fresh bean sprouts
- 1 lime, cut into wedges

Instructions

1. In a medium saucepan combine sugar, vinegar, soy sauce and tamarind pulp over medium heat.
2. Soak rice noodles in cold water until soft. Drain. In a large skillet or wok warm oil and add garlic and eggs over medium heat. Add and scramble the eggs. Add tofu and stir until well mixed. Add noodles and stir until fully cooked.
3. Stir in sauce mixture, 1 1/2 tablespoons sugar and 1 1/2 teaspoons salt. Stir in peanuts and ground radish. Remove from heat and add chives and paprika.
4. Serve with lime and bean sprouts.

Veggie Lo Mein

SERVINGS: 6
PREP TIME: 15 min.
TOTAL TIME: 25 min.

Ingredients

- 1 pound dry Chinese noodles
- 1 cup chopped fresh mushrooms
- 1 (8 ounce) can bamboo shoots, drained
- 1 cup chopped celery
- 1 cup bean sprouts
- 1/2 teaspoon chopped garlic
- 1 teaspoon salt
- 1 cup vegetable broth
- 1 teaspoon white sugar
- 1 cup water
- 1 tablespoon soy sauce
- 1 tablespoon oyster sauce
- 1 tablespoon all-purpose flour

Instructions

1. Bring a large pot of lightly salted water to a boil. Add Chinese noodles and cook about 2 to 4 minutes. Drain.
2. In a large skillet or wok add small amount of oil over high heat. Cook mushrooms, bamboo shoots, celery, bean sprouts and garlic. Mix in salt, broth, sugar, water, soy sauce and oyster sauce, occasionally stir. Add flour and cook until thickened.
3. Pour over noodles and lightly toss.

Thai Peanut Noodles

SERVINGS: 4
PREP TIME: 15 min.
TOTAL TIME: 35 min.

Ingredients

- 1 (8 ounce) package uncooked spaghetti
- 1 tablespoon corn-starch
- 1 cup vegetable broth
- 1/3 cup creamy peanut butter
- 3 tablespoons soy sauce
- 3 tablespoons honey
- 3 tablespoons brown sugar
- 1 teaspoon sesame oil
- 1 teaspoon ground ginger
- 1/4 teaspoon ground red pepper
- 2 tablespoons sake
- 2 tablespoons vegetable oil
- 2 cloves garlic, minced
- 1 onion, chopped
- 1 cup broccoli florets
- 1 cup carrots, sliced
- 1/2 cup red bell pepper, chopped
- 1/2 cup sugar snap peas

Instructions

1. Fill a large pot with lightly salted water. Bring to a boil over high heat. Stir in the spaghetti and cook the pasta uncovered, occasionally stirring, for about 12 minutes, or until the pasta has cooked through but is still firm. Drain set aside.
2. Whisk corn-starch into vegetable broth until dissolved. Add and whisk in peanut butter, soy sauce, honey, brown sugar, sesame oil, ground ginger, and red pepper. In a skillet, bring to a boil over medium-high heat. Reduce heat to medium-low, and simmer for about 5 minutes until thickened. Stir in sake and keep warm.
3. In a large skillet, heat vegetable oil over medium heat. Stir in the garlic and onion; cooking and stirring about 5 minutes or until

onion has softened and turned translucent. Stir in the broccoli, carrots, red bell pepper, and sugar snap peas. Reduce heat, cover, and steam for about 5 minutes, or until the vegetables are tender.

4. Toss vegetables with the peanut sauce and pasta to serve.

Lemon Coconut Thai Pasta

SERVINGS: 4
PREP TIME: 25 min.
TOTAL TIME: 45 min.

Ingredients

- 1/2 (8 ounce) package spaghetti
- 1 cup coconut milk
- 1/2 cup dry white wine
- 1/4 cup fresh lemon juice
- 2 tablespoons olive oil
- 3 cloves garlic, minced, or more to taste
- 1 teaspoon white sugar (optional)
- 1/4 teaspoon salt
- 1/8 teaspoon red pepper flakes
- 1/8 teaspoon ground black pepper
- 2 Roma (plum) tomatoes, diced
- 1/2 cup bean sprouts
- 1/4 cup chopped fresh basil
- 1/4 cup chopped fresh parsley
- 3 green onions, chopped
- 1 (5 ounce) package arugula
- 1 lemon, zested

Instructions

1. Boil a large pot of lightly salted water. Cook spaghetti in the boiling water, 12 minutes, or until cooked through but firm to the bite, stirring occasionally. Drain and return spaghetti to pot.
2. In a small saucepan, whisk coconut milk, white wine, lemon juice, olive oil, garlic, sugar, salt, red pepper flakes, and black pepper over medium heat. Simmer 5 to 6 minutes or until flavors combine.
3. Combine tomatoes, bean sprouts, basil, parsley, and green onions in pasta. Cook 3 to 5 minutes over low heat until warmed through. Mix in coconut sauce.
4. Serve pasta over arugula. Sprinkle with lemon zest.

Vietnamese Pesto Pasta

SERVINGS: 4
PREP TIME: 20 min.
TOTAL TIME: 35 min.

Ingredients

- 1 pound dried rice noodles
- 1 1/2 cups chopped fresh cilantro
- 1/2 cup sweet Thai basil
- 2 cloves garlic, halved
- 1/2 teaspoon minced lemon grass bulb
- 1 jalapeno pepper, seeded and minced
- 1 tablespoon vegetarian fish sauce
- 4 tablespoons chopped, unsalted dry-roasted peanuts
- 7 tablespoons canola oil
- 1/2 lime, cut into wedges
- salt and pepper to taste

Instructions

1. In a large bowl of cold water, soak rice noodles for 30 minutes. Drain and set them aside.
2. In a food processor or blender combine chopped cilantro, basil, garlic cloves, lemongrass, jalapeno peppers, imitation fish sauce or salt, and 2 tablespoons of peanuts. Coarsely chop the herbs and peanuts. During blending, add the oil in a thin stream. Add remaining peanuts, pulsing until peanuts are coarsely chopped.
3. In a large skillet, over medium-high heat place rice noodles with 1/2 cup water. Stir until the noodles are tender and water is mostly absorbed.
4. Add nearly all the pesto, and stir well. Add a few tablespoons of water if the pesto clumps.
5. Add more pesto to the pasta, lime juice, fish sauce, salt, or pepper if desired. Garnish with the remaining 2 tablespoons of peanuts.

Sesame Tofu Linguine

SERVINGS: 6
PREP TIME: 15 min.
TOTAL TIME: 45 min.

Ingredients

- 6 tablespoons vegetable oil
- 2 cloves garlic, chopped
- 6 tablespoons soy sauce
- 6 tablespoons rice vinegar
- 1 tablespoon Thai chili sauce
- 3 tablespoons honey
- 8 ounces extra-firm tofu, cut into 1/4-inch cubes
- 1/2 (16 ounce) package linguine pasta
- 1 tablespoon sesame oil
- 8 ounces bean sprouts
- 8 ounces shredded carrots
- 1 green bell pepper, thinly sliced
- 8 green onions, halved lengthwise

Instructions

1. Heat the vegetable oil over medium-high heat in a wok or skillet. Add and stir in the garlic about 2 minutes, or until lightly browned. Pour in soy sauce, rice vinegar, chili sauce, and honey. Stir and bring to a simmer. Reduce heat to medium-low and simmer for 10 minutes. Transfer sauce to a bowl and stir tofu in. Set aside.
2. Boil lightly salted water in a large pot over high heat. Once boiling, stir in the linguine. Cook uncovered for about 11 minutes, stirring occasionally until pasta is cooked but firm. Drain and set in the sink.
3. While the pasta is boiling, heat the sesame oil in clean wok or large skillet; cook and stir the bean sprouts, carrots, green pepper, and green onions until the vegetables are bright in color and slightly wilted, about 5 minutes. Pour in the tofu with sauce and linguine. Stir together and serve.

Toasted Sesame Seed Soba

SERVINGS: 4
PREP/TOTAL TIME: 45 min.

Ingredients

- 1/2 cup sesame seeds
- 8 ounces dried soba noodles
- 2 tablespoons balsamic vinegar
- 1 tablespoon white sugar
- 2 1/2 tablespoons soy sauce
- 1 clove garlic, minced
- 1 teaspoon dark sesame oil
- 5 green onions, chopped
- 3 cups broccoli florets

Instructions

1. Preheat oven to 375 degrees F (190 degrees C).
2. Pour sesame seeds onto a baking sheet. Toast the seeds in the oven for 10 to 12 minutes, until brown around the edges.
3. Boil a large pot of salted water. Add noodles and cook for 5 to 6 minutes, or until tender. Drain, rinse well with cold water, and drain again.
4. Mix the vinegar, sugar, soy sauce, garlic, sesame oil and green onions together in a large mixing bowl. Add noodles and the toasted sesame seeds. Toss well, and stir in the broccoli.
5. Let sit for 30 minutes at room temperature before serving.

CURRY

Green Curry Tofu

SERVINGS: 4
PREP/TOTAL TIME: 45 min.

Ingredients

- 1 1/2 cups water
- 1 cup uncooked basmati rice, rinsed and drained
- 3 tablespoons sesame oil
- 1 (14 ounce) package firm water-packed tofu, drained and cubed
- 1/4 teaspoon salt
- 1 (10 ounce) can coconut milk
- 2 tablespoons green curry paste

Instructions

1. In a medium saucepan, pour water, stir in rice, and bring to a boil. Cover, reduce heat, and simmer for 20 minutes. Remove from heat, cool, and fluff with a fork.
2. In a separate medium saucepan, heat sesame oil over medium heat. Stir in tofu and cook for about 20 minutes, until evenly crisp and lightly browned, stirring occasionally. Season with salt.
3. Bring coconut milk to a boil in a small saucepan. Mix in green curry paste. Reduce heat, and simmer 5 minutes. Pour over tofu and rice.

Spinach, Red Lentil, and Bean Curry

SERVINGS: 4
PREP TIME: 15 min.
TOTAL TIME: 40 min.

Ingredients

- 1 cup red lentils
- 1/4 cup tomato puree
- 1/2 (8 ounce) container plain yogurt
- 1 teaspoon garam masala
- 1/2 teaspoon ground dried turmeric
- 1/2 teaspoon ground cumin
- 1/2 teaspoon ancho chile powder
- 2 tablespoons vegetable oil
- 1 onion, chopped
- 2 cloves garlic, chopped
- 1 (1 inch) piece fresh ginger root, grated
- 4 cups loosely packed fresh spinach, coarsely chopped
- 2 tomatoes, chopped
- 4 sprigs fresh cilantro, chopped
- 1 (15.5 ounce) can mixed beans, rinsed and drained

Instructions

1. Rinse lentils and place in a saucepan. Cover with water and bring to a boil. Reduce heat to low and cover pot. Simmer over low heat for 20 minutes. Drain.
2. In a bowl, stir together tomato puree and yogurt. Season with garam masala, turmeric, cumin, and chile powder. Stir until creamy.
3. Heat oil over medium heat in a skillet. Stir in onion, garlic, and ginger, cooing until onion browns. Stir in spinach and cook until it turns wilted and dark green. Gradually stir in the yogurt mixture and add in tomatoes and cilantro.
4. Stir lentils and mixed beans into mixture until well mixed. Cook for about 5 minutes, until heated through.

Tofu and Potatoes Coconut Curry

SERVINGS: 4
PREP TIME: 15 min.
TOTAL TIME: 45 min.

Ingredients

- 4 slices fresh ginger root
- 4 cloves garlic, minced
- 1/4 cup cashews
- 2 stalks lemon grass, chopped
- 2 onions, sliced
- 3 tablespoons olive oil
- 1 dash crushed red pepper flakes
- 2 tablespoons curry powder
- 2 1/2 cups cubed firm tofu
- 1 (14 ounce) can coconut milk
- 14 fluid ounces water
- 2 medium potatoes, peeled and cubed
- 2 teaspoons salt
- 1 tablespoon white sugar

Instructions

1. In a blender or food processor, grind the ginger root, garlic, cashews, lemon grass, and onions into a paste.
2. Heat olive oil in a medium wok over low heat. Stir in the blended mixture and red pepper flakes. Gradually mix in the curry powder.
3. Place tofu in the wok, and cook until heated through. Mix in the coconut milk, water, and potatoes. Bring to a boil, reduce heat, and simmer 20 minutes, stirring occasionally, until potatoes are tender. Season with salt and sugar.

Coconut Curry Tofu

SERVINGS: 6
PREP TIME: 15 min.
TOTAL TIME: 25 min.

Ingredients

- 2 bunches green onions
- 1 (14 ounce) can light coconut milk
- 1/4 cup soy sauce, divided
- 1/2 teaspoon brown sugar
- 1 1/2 teaspoons curry powder
- 1 teaspoon minced fresh ginger
- 2 teaspoons chile paste
- 1 pound firm tofu, cut into 3/4 inch cubes
- 4 Roma (plum) tomatoes, chopped
- 1 yellow bell pepper, thinly sliced
- 4 ounces fresh mushrooms, chopped
- 1/4 cup chopped fresh basil
- 4 cups chopped bok choy
- salt to taste

Instructions

1. Remove the white parts of the green onion. Finely chop into 2 inch pieces.
2. In a large heavy skillet mix coconut milk, 3 tablespoons soy sauce, brown sugar, curry powder, ginger, and chile paste over medium heat. Bring to a boil.
3. In the skillet, stir tofu, tomatoes, yellow pepper, mushrooms, and finely chopped green onions. Cover, and cook for 5 minutes, occasionally stirring. Mix in basil and bok choy, and season with salt and remaining soy sauce. Cook for 5 minutes, or until vegetables are crisp but tender.
4. Garnish with green onion.

Thai Green Curry with Spring Vegetables

SERVINGS: 2-4
PREP TIME: 15 min.
TOTAL TIME: 45 min.

Ingredients

- 1 cup brown basmati rice, rinsed
- 2 teaspoons coconut oil or olive oil
- 1 small white onion, diced
- 1 tablespoon (about a 1-inch) finely chopped fresh ginger, peeled and chopped)
- 2 cloves garlic, finely chopped
- Pinch of salt
- 1/2 bunch asparagus (about 2 cups), tough ends removed and sliced in 2-inch long pieces
- 3 carrots, peeled and sliced diagonally in 1/4-inch wide rounds (1 cup sliced carrots)
- 2 tablespoons Thai green curry paste
- 1 can (14 ounces) coconut milk
- 1/2 cup water
- 1 1/2 teaspoons coconut sugar, turbinado (raw) sugar, or brown sugar
- 2 cups packed baby spinach, roughly chopped
- 1 1/2 teaspoons rice vinegar
- 1 1/2 teaspoons soy sauce
- Handful of chopped fresh cilantro and red pepper flakes, if desired

Instructions

1. Boil a large pot of water. Add rinsed rice and boil for 30 minutes, reduce heat when necessary to avoid overflow. Remove from heat, drain rice and return the rice to pot. Cover and let stand for at least 10 minutes, until you're ready to serve.
2. In a large skillet, warm a couple of teaspoons of oil over medium heat. Cook onion, ginger, and garlic with a sprinkle of salt for about 5 minutes, stirring frequently. Add asparagus and carrots and

cook for 3 minutes more, occasionally stirring. Add the curry paste and cook, for 2 minutes, stirring frequently.

3. Add in coconut milk, 1/2 cup water, and 1 1/2 teaspoons sugar. Bring mixture to a simmer. Maintain a simmer and cook about 5 to 10 minutes, or until carrots and asparagus are cooked and tender.

4. Stir in the spinach and cook about 30 seconds or until the spinach has wilted. Remove curry from heat and season with rice vinegar and soy sauce. Add salt and red pepper flakes, to taste.

5. Divide rice and curry into bowls and garnish with cilantro and a red pepper flakes, if desired.

Lime-Curry Tofu Stir-Fry

SERVINGS: 4
PREP TIME: 10 min.
TOTAL TIME: 30 min.

Ingredients

- 2 tablespoons peanut oil
- 1 (16 ounce) package extra-firm tofu, cut into bite-sized cubes
- 1 tablespoon minced fresh ginger root
- 2 tablespoons red curry paste
- 1 pound zucchini, diced 1 red bell pepper, diced
- 3 tablespoons lime juice
- 3 tablespoons soy sauce
- 2 tablespoons maple syrup
- 1 (14 ounce) can coconut milk
- 1/2 cup chopped fresh basil

Instructions

1. In a wok or large skillet, heat peanut oil over high heat. Add tofu and stir-fry until golden brown. Remove tofu and set aside, leaving the oil in the wok.
2. In the hot oil, stir in ginger and curry paste for a few seconds until ginger turns golden and the curry paste is fragrant. Add zucchini and bell pepper, cooking and stirring for 1 minute. Pour in the lime juice, soy sauce, maple syrup, coconut milk, and tofu. Bring coconut milk to a simmer, and cook until the tofu is hot and vegetables are tender.
3. Stir in chopped basil before serving.

APPETIZERS

Spicy Eggplant

SERVINGS: 6
PREP TIME: 20 min.
TOTAL TIME: 15 min.

Ingredients

- 2 tablespoons vegetable oil
- 4 Japanese eggplants, cut into 1-inch cubes
- 2 tablespoons vegetable oil
- 2 onions, thinly sliced
- 1 tablespoon minced garlic
- 2 tablespoons soy sauce
- 2 tablespoons water
- 1 1/2 tablespoons oyster sauce
- 1 tablespoon chili garlic sauce
- 1 teaspoon white sugar
- ground black pepper to taste
- 1/2 teaspoon Asian (toasted) sesame oil

Instructions

1. In a large skillet or wok, heat 2 tablespoons of oil over medium-high heat until almost smoking. Cook and stir eggplant, 3 to 5 minutes or until they begin to brown. Remove with a slotted spoon. Set aside.
2. In the skillet over medium-high heat, cook 2 more tablespoons of oil. Stir in onions about 30 seconds just until they begin to soften. Stir in garlic, and cook for 30 seconds. Mix in soy sauce, water, oyster sauce, chili garlic sauce, sugar, and black pepper, and until mixture is smooth.
3. Return eggplant to the skillet, lower heat, and let simmer, about 5 minutes or until eggplant is tender and nearly all the liquid has been absorbed.
4. Drizzle sesame oil over the dish and stir to combine.

Marinated Portobello Mushrooms

SERVINGS: 2
PREP TIME: 10 min.
TOTAL TIME: 1 hour

Ingredients

- 1/2 cup cooking wine
- 1 tablespoon olive oil
- 2 tablespoons dark soy sauce
- 2 tablespoons balsamic vinegar
- 2 cloves garlic, minced
- 2 large Portobello mushroom caps

Instructions

1. Preheat oven to 400 degrees F (200 degrees C).
2. Mix the wine, olive oil, soy sauce, balsamic vinegar, and garlic in a baking dish. Place mushroom upside down in marinade, and let marinate for 15 minutes.
3. Cover dish, and transfer to oven, baking for 25 minutes.
4. Turn mushrooms and continue baking another 8 minutes.

Banh-Mi Vietnamese Baguette

SERVINGS: 2
PREP TIME: 20 min.
TOTAL TIME: 45 min.

Ingredients

- 2 Portobello mushroom caps, sliced
- 2 teaspoons olive oil
- salt and pepper, to taste
- 1 carrot, sliced into sticks
- 1 daikon (white) radish, sliced into sticks
- 1 cup rice vinegar
- 1/2 cup fresh lime juice
- 1/2 cup cold water
- 1/2 cup chilled lime juice
- 2 teaspoons soy sauce
- 1 teaspoon vegetarian fish sauce
- 1/2 teaspoon toasted sesame oil
- 2 tablespoons canola oil
- 2 teaspoons minced garlic
- 1/3 cup white sugar
- 1/3 cup cold water
- 1 jalapeno pepper, thinly sliced
- 8 sprigs fresh cilantro with stems
- 1 medium cucumber, sliced into thin strips
- 2 sprigs fresh Thai basil
- 2 (7 inch) French bread baguettes, split lengthwise

Instructions

1. Preheat the oven to 450 degrees F (230 degrees C). Place mushrooms on a baking sheet. Drizzle with some olive oil and season with salt and pepper. Roast in oven for about 25 minutes. Cool slightly, and slice into strips.
2. During roasting, boil a saucepan of water. Place carrot and radish sticks into boiling water for a few seconds. Remove them and plunge into a bowl of ice water.

3. In a different bowl, stir rice vinegar, 1/2 cup of lime juice and 1/2 cup cold water. Transfer carrot and radish to the vinegar and lime marinade and let soak for at least 15 minutes.
4. For the sandwich sauce, stir together the remaining lime juice, soy sauce, fish sauce, sesame oil, canola oil, 1/3 cup sugar and 1/3 cup water in a small bowl.
5. Sprinkle some of the sauce onto each half of the French loaves. Place the roasted mushrooms onto the bottom of each roll and sprinkle with some more sauce.
6. Top with some jalapeno, carrot and radish (without the marinade), cucumber, basil and cilantro. Close with the tops of the bread. Serve.

Thai Stuffed Tofu

SERVINGS: 4
PREP TIME: 20 min.
TOTAL TIME: 45 min.

Ingredients

- 2 (12 ounce) packages extra firm tofu
- 1/4 cup dried shiitake mushrooms
- 1 zucchini, coarsely chopped
- 1 onion, halved
- 3 cloves garlic
- 1 jalapeno pepper, seeded and coarsely chopped
- 1 egg
- 2 tablespoons soy sauce
- 2 tablespoons minced fresh ginger, or to taste
- 1 tablespoon corn-starch
- 1 tablespoon hoisin sauce
- 1/4 cup shredded cabbage
- 1/4 cup vegetable oil, divided

Instructions

1. Drain tofu and cut into 4 squares, and then cut each square diagonally into 2 triangles. Set aside.
2. In a bowl of hot water, place shiitake mushrooms for about 20 minutes or until rehydrated and plump. Cut out stems and finely chop.
3. In a food processor, blend zucchini, onion, garlic, and jalapeno pepper until vegetables are almost a paste. Transfer to a bowl and stir in shiitake mushrooms, egg, soy sauce, ginger, corn-starch, and hoisin sauce. Fold shredded cabbage into the stuffing.
4. In a large skillet, heat 2 tablespoons vegetable oil over medium heat. With paper towels, pat tofu dry. Pan-fry in the hot oil until browned except narrow side, about 2 to 3 minutes frying per side. Remove tofu and let cool.
5. With a knife, cut a slit into the unbrowned side of a tofu. Scoop center of tofu with a spoon, and leave the walls about 1/4-inch thick. Use a spoon to fill each tofu piece with the stuffing.

6. In a skillet, heat remaining 2 tablespoons vegetable oil over medium heat. Place tofu triangles, stuffing sides down, into the hot oil and pan-fry until edge is browned, about 5 minutes or stuffing is hot and has set inside. Turn tofu on their sides and refry for a minute or two in the hot oil to rewarm.

Green Onion Cakes

SERVINGS: 8
PREP TIME: 20 min.
TOTAL TIME: 1 hour 20 min

Ingredients

- 3 cups bread flour
- 1 1/4 cups boiling water
- 2 tablespoons vegetable oil
- salt and pepper to taste
- 1 bunch green onions, finely chopped
- 2 teaspoons vegetable oil

Instructions

1. In a large bowl, mix flour and boiling water. Form dough into a ball. Cover bowl with plastic wrap and let dough rest for 30 to 60 minutes.
2. Divide dough evenly into 16 pieces. Roll each piece into a 1/4 inch thick circle. Brush each piece with oil, season with salt and pepper, and sprinkle 1 teaspoon of green onions. Roll up like a cigar and pinch open ends to form a circle. Roll each circle flat to 1/4 inch.
3. Heat 2 teaspoons oil in a large skillet. Fry about 2 minutes on each side, or until golden brown.

Teriyaki Pineapple

SERVINGS: 4
PREP TIME: 20 min.
TOTAL TIME: 30 min. + refrigeration

Ingredients

- 1 (12 ounce) package firm tofu
- 1 cup chopped fresh pineapple
- 2 cups teriyaki sauce

Instructions

1. Cut tofu into bite sized pieces and place it in a deep baking dish. Add pineapple and pour in teriyaki sauce. Refrigerate for at least 1 hour.
2. Preheat oven to 350 degrees F (175 degrees C).
3. Bake in oven for 20 minutes, or until bubbly and hot.

Vietnamese Omelette Pancakes

SERVINGS: 4
PREP TIME: 20 min.
TOTAL TIME: 30 min.

Ingredients

Sauce
- 1 1/2 tablespoons hoisin sauce
- 1 tablespoon low-sodium soy sauce
- 1 tablespoons crushed roasted peanuts
- 1 1/2 teaspoons ketchup
- 1/2 teaspoons rice vinegar
- 1/4 teaspoons chile-garlic sauce
Pancakes
- 1/2 cup brown rice flour
- 2 tablespoons corn-starch
- 2 tablespoons cake flour
- 2 green onions, sliced (1/4 cup), divided
- 4 teaspoons toasted sesame oil
- 4 oz. soft tofu, drained and thinly sliced
- 1 cup sliced mushrooms
- 2 large eggs, beaten
- 1 cup bean sprouts
- 1/2 cup chopped fresh watercress
- 1/2 cup chopped fresh mint
- 1/2 cup chopped Thai or sweet basil leaves

Instructions

1. In a bowl, whisk together all sauce ingredients with 1 tablespoon of water. Set aside.
2. In another bowl, whisk rice flour, corn-starch, and cake flour. Add 1 cup water and whisk until smooth. Stir in 2 tablespoons of green onion.
3. In 10-inch non-stick skillet, heat 2 teaspoons of oil over medium-high heat. Add 3/4 cup batter, and tilt the skillet to coat pan bottom completely with batter. Reduce heat to medium-low. Arrange 2 oz.

tofu and 1/2 cup mushrooms on top of the pancake, and scatter with 1/4 cup beaten egg. Cover, and cook for 5 minutes.

4. Uncover skillet, and drizzle 1/2 cup bean sprouts over mixture. Cook 3 more minutes, or until the bottom is golden and crispy.

5. Scatter 1/4 cup watercress, 1/4 cup mint, 1/4 cup basil, and 1 tablespoon of green onions over bean sprouts. Fold pancake in half, like an omelette, and slide onto plate.

6. Repeat to make more pancakes. Serve with sauce on side.

Barb-a-Fu

SERVINGS: 3
PREP TIME: 15 min.
TOTAL TIME: 45 min.

Ingredients

- 3 tablespoons cornmeal
- 1 tablespoon all-purpose flour
- 1/8 teaspoon crushed red pepper flakes, or to taste
- 1 teaspoon garlic powder, or to taste
- 1/4 teaspoon chili powder, or to taste
- salt and pepper to taste
- 1 (12 ounce) package extra-firm tofu, cut into 1/4-inch thick slices
- 1 tablespoon olive oil
- 1/4 cup minced onion
- 1 teaspoon soy sauce
- 3/4 cup barbeque sauce

Instructions

1. Spray a 9x13-inch baking dish with cooking spray. Preheat oven to 350 degrees F (175 degrees C).
2. In a resealable plastic bag, place cornmeal, flour, red pepper flakes, garlic powder, chili powder, salt, and pepper. Shake to mix. Gently shake tofu with cornmeal mix to coat, shake off excess, and place into baking dish.
3. Bake tofu in oven for 10 minutes, then turn pieces over and to cook for 10 more minutes.
4. In a saucepan, heat olive oil over medium heat. Add minced onion and cook about 3 minutes or until translucent. Stir in soy sauce and barbeque sauce. Bring to a simmer, turn heat to low, and keep warm.
5. When tofu has cooked, pour hot barbeque sauce over the top. Return to the oven and bake for 5 more minutes.

Hot Beans in Coconut Milk

SERVINGS: 6
PREP TIME: 30 min.
TOTAL TIME: 1 hour 20 min

Ingredients

- 1 (14 ounce) can coconut milk
- 4 tablespoons minced fresh ginger root
- 3 cloves garlic, minced
- 2 tablespoons chopped fresh parsley
- 1 teaspoon salt
- 2 teaspoons ground turmeric
- 2 teaspoons ground cumin
- 2 tablespoons chili powder
- 1 tablespoon curry paste
- 1 (14.5 ounce) can black beans, drained and rinsed
- 1 (14.5 ounce) can kidney beans, drained and rinsed
- 1/2 red bell pepper, chopped
- 1/2 green bell pepper, chopped

Instructions

1. In a deep skillet, combine the coconut milk, ginger, garlic, and parsley over medium heat. Season with salt, turmeric, cumin, chili powder, and curry paste. Bring to a slow boil.
2. Stir in black beans, kidney beans, and red and green bell peppers. Let simmer, stirring occasionally, about 30 to 45 minutes or until the sauce is thick and 1/3 of the liquid has evaporated. Cover, remove from heat and let cool for 5 to 10 minutes.

THANK YOU

Thank you for checking out Quick and Easy Asian Vegetarian Meals. I hope you enjoyed these recipes as much as I have. I am always looking for feedback on how to improve, so if you have any questions, suggestions, or comments please send me an email at susan.evans.author@gmail.com. Also, if you enjoyed the book would you consider leaving on honest review? As a new author, they help me out in a big way. Thanks again, and have fun cooking!

Other popular books by Susan Evans

Vegetarian Mediterranean Cookbook:
Over 50 recipes for appetizers, salads, dips, and main dishes

Vegetarian Slow Cooker Cookbook:
Over 75 recipes for meals, soups, stews, desserts, and sides

Quick & Easy Vegan Desserts Cookbook:
Over 80 delicious recipes for cakes, cupcakes, brownies, cookies, fudge, pies, candy, and so much more!

Quick & Easy Vegetarian Rice Cooker Meals:
Over 50 recipes for breakfast, main dishes, and desserts

Quick & Easy Rice Cooker Meals:
Over 60 recipes for breakfast, main dishes, soups, and desserts

Quick & Easy Microwave Meals:
Over 50 recipes for breakfast, snacks, meals and desserts

Halloween Cookbook:
80 Ghoulish recipes for appetizers, meals, drinks, and desserts

Printed in Great Britain
by Amazon